TOAK TREE

GORDON MORRISON

HOUGHTON MIFFLIN COMPANY BOSTON 2000

Walter Lorraine Books

To my children Suzanne, Seth and Aimee
with a wish for a soft patch of soil in which to set their roots
and to their grandmother, Martha Grace,
I dedicate this book with love and affection.

Walter Lorraine 〰 Books

Copyright © 2000 by Gordon Morrison

Library of Congress Cataloging-in-Publication Data

Morrison, Gordon,
    Oak tree / by Gordon Morrison.
        p.   cm.
    Summary: Describes the impact of the changing seasons on an old
oak tree and the life that surrounds it.
    ISBN 0-395-95644-7
    1. Oak — Juvenile literature.   2. Oak — Ecology — Juvenile
literature.   3. Animal-plant relationships — Juvenile literature.
4. Seasons — Juvenile literature.   [1. Oak. 2. Trees. 3. Forest
ecology. 4. Ecology. 5. Seasons.]   I. Title.
QK495.F14M67   2000
583'.46—dc21   98-55148
                                                    CIP

Printed in the United States of America
WOZ 10 9 8 7 6 5 4 3 2 1

Every day for
many weeks now,
the sun has risen a
little higher in the sky.
Each day is longer and
warmer than the day before.
On this day something special happens.
An old oak tree, warmed by the rising sun,
slowly wakes from a long winter's rest —
spring has arrived.

The old tree moves sap water from its roots
and stem to its twigs and buds. Fed by the sap,
the buds slowly grow plump and lengthen.

A mourning cloak butterfly crawls from a
crack in the oak tree's bark, spreads
its wings in the warm sun,
and flutters away.

Meanwhile, near the top of the
tree, a red-tailed hawk has
returned to its nest. Soon its
mate will return, and they
will once again raise a family.

Mourning cloak butterfly.
This butterfly is one of
only a few insects that spend
the winter as an adult.
In late fall the butterfly
crawls into a crevice.
In spring it emerges,
mates, and lays its eggs.
Caterpillars hatch from the
eggs. After the caterpillar
grows, it forms a covering
called a chrysalis, from
which, in late summer, an
adult butterfly will emerge.

Three or four weeks pass.
The buds split open,
and small leaves and
flowers push out.
Caterpillars chew on
the young leaves.

Red-tailed hawk.
A large bird of prey, 19 to 25 inches long.
May use the same nest year after year.
Breeds in April. Raises two to
three young. Young leave the nest
by August. Migrate in October.

Oak flowers. Oaks depend on the wind to spread their pollen. Male flowers produce pollen. Female flowers receive pollen and develop acorns. Pollen is a fine material, like dust, that is used by flowers in fertilization.

A pollen grain, greatly magnified.

The flowers grow quickly. A week later, the tree is in full bloom. The oak has two kinds of flowers, male and female. The male flowers hang from long thin stems that sway in the wind and drop a dust called pollen. The female flowers grow at the bases of the leaves and are sprinkled by the pollen dust.

A pair of downy woodpeckers takes turns chipping wood from one of the oak's large limbs. They are making a nest hole where they will raise their family. The female pauses in her work to eat a caterpillar.

During the weeks when the oak tree
flowers, a pair of robins builds a
nest on the tree's branches.
After the flowers drop their
pollen and fall from the twigs,
the female robin settles
into the nest
to lay her eggs.

Downy woodpecker.
5 to 6 inches long.
A bird adapted for chipping wood.
This woodpecker takes as long
as three weeks to chip a hole
for use as a nest cavity.
Drills into wood for insects.
Drums on wood to declare its
territory or call its mate.
Begins courtship in late winter.
Lays three to five eggs in late May.

American robin.
9 to 11 inches long. A well-known member
of the thrush family. Commonly
seen on lawns looking for worms.
A robin often builds its nest
on the fork of a horizontal
branch. Lays four sky-blue
eggs in early May. Usually has
two broods, sometimes three.
First brood leaves nest in June.

Days pass and continue to grow
longer and warmer.
Small knobs now grow
at the base of each leaf where
the female flowers used to be.
These knobs are young acorns.
A gray squirrel scurries up the oak's
trunk. It is carrying a cluster of dry
leaves to its leaf nest high in the tree.
On the other side of the trunk, honeybees
fly to and from their hive in the tree.
The back legs of the returning bees
are covered with pollen and nectar.

Gray squirrel.
15 to 20 inches long. This squirrel builds
a nest of dry leaves and live leaf clusters
in a tree crotch or hole of a tree.
Up to six young are born in spring, the
first of two litters. The gray squirrel
buries acorns in fall as a winter food cache.
Acorns that are not later recovered
by the squirrels may sprout and grow
into trees.

Honeybees.
Many plants depend on honeybees and other insects,
rather than wind, to
spread their pollen.
Flying from flower to
flower, bees gather
nectar and pollen
on their hind legs.
Some pollen brushes
off on the next flower
they visit, fertilizing it.
Bees make honey
from nectar and store it
in the hive for food. The hive is
home to thousands of bees.

More leaves appear every day.
They spread to catch as much
sunlight as they can. The oak
uses the sunlight to make food
in its leaves to help it grow.
This process is photosynthesis
(foe-toe-sin-tha-sis).

Photosynthesis.
The process by which green plants use
sunlight to combine carbon dioxide,
water, and chlorophyll to make the
tree's food supply.

Sunlight is the source of energy
that draws water from the tree
into the leaves, where carbon dioxide
(from the air) combines with
chlorophyll (in the leaves) to make
dextrose (sugar).

Stomata are the tiny pores on the
undersides of leaves that let
moisture out of the leaf and air in.

Chlorophyll, a green substance
found in leaf cells, is essential to
photosynthesis. Chlorophyll gives
leaves their green color.

Dextrose (sugar) and water make
sap, the food used by the tree
for all its growth needs.

The parts of the tree below ground. The roots anchor the tree in place and absorb water and nutrients. The entire root system may spread as much below ground as the tree does above ground.

Root tip: the growing end of a root. Root tips are threadlike in appearance. There may be millions of root tips in a mature oak, each twisting and probing into the soil.

Root hairs: minute hairs grow from each root tip. Hundreds of hairs on each tip absorb water and nutrients from the soil, supplying all the tree's needs. As the root tip continues to grow and burrow, older hairs stop absorbing and die. As it grows into a mature root, that portion of the tip now conducts water and nutrients up to the tree.

Root cap: a covering that protects the root tip as it burrows through the soil. The area directly behind the cap is the only part of the root that grows in length.

The old tree's roots reach deep into the soil and secure the tree in the ground. Under the roots are spaces where some animals find shelter. A skunk family has a den in a hollow under one of the oak's huge roots. The mother skunk scolds a hognose snake that has come too near her home. The hognose spreads its head, puffs its body, and hisses in defense. The skunk does not attack, and the lucky snake slowly backs away. It will look somewhere else for a place to lay its eggs.

Striped skunk.
25 to 30 inches long. This skunk may dig its own burrow, but often takes over the den of another animal. In self-defense, skunks spray a foul-smelling fluid from glands near the base of their tail. Before squirting, however, they give a warning by raising their tail and stamping their feet. Skunks eat a variety of things, including nuts, insects, turtle eggs, and hognose snakes.

Hognose snake.
Up to 36 inches long. It lays its eggs in early summer in loose, damp soil. It is so named because of its upturned snout, which it uses to burrow and search for food. When threatened, the snake puts on a cobra-like defense display. It will even strike, but it rarely bites. If this fails, the snake rolls onto its back and plays dead. If turned upright, it will roll onto its back again.

By midsummer,
the old oak has spread
most of its leaves.
The robins are raising
their second family.
High in the oak a gray tree frog
perches on a branch and sings
its song, a birdlike trill.

Gray tree frog.
To 2½ inches long. Tree frogs have sticky disks on their toes for climbing
and clinging. They climb trees in summer after spending the spring breeding
season in or near water. They eat insects that they catch with their sticky
tongue. Tree frogs are difficult to see in their surroundings because they
camouflage — they change color to match their environment,
from gray to green or brown.

Late on a hot
summer night,
a male tree cricket
clings to the oak's bark
and sings its song.
The female cricket hears
his call and crawls up
the bark toward him.

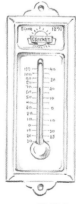

Tree cricket.
⅝ inch long.
This cricket is most active
at night in late summer.
Males call to attract mates.
Females lay forty to fifty eggs on bark.
Eggs survive winter and hatch into tiny
crickets that mature and mate by summer's end.
Eggs are laid and adult crickets die off in the cold weather.
Folklore: count the number of times a tree cricket calls in fifteen seconds, then
add thirty-seven. The result will equal the approximate temperature in degrees
Fahrenheit.

On the longest, hottest days of summer, shade from the oak's leaves helps to cool the birds, mammals, and insects that live on, in, and around the tree.

Transpiration.
The movement of water throughout the tree. Water is found in all parts of the tree. Without water, a tree cannot survive.

Sunlight evaporates water in the leaves and draws water from the branches and trunk, causing an upward flow from the roots that draws water molecules (and nutrients) from the surrounding soil.

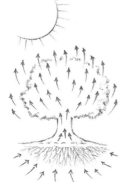

Tree topography.
Crown: a tree's full width and height above its trunk.
Foliage: a leaf cluster or the mass of a tree's leaves.
Twigs: small branches on which most branching and budding occur.
Branches: support twigs and move sap.
Limbs: the largest branches.
Trunk: the tree's main support above ground.
Roots: the part of the tree that grows under the ground.

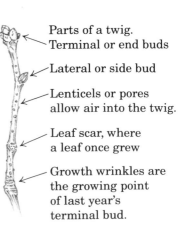

Parts of a twig.
Terminal or end buds

Lateral or side bud

Lenticels or pores allow air into the twig.

Leaf scar, where a leaf once grew

Growth wrinkles are the growing point of last year's terminal bud.

By the end of summer, the acorn knobs
have grown into capped nuts,
and small buds have grown
at the base of many leaves.
Inside each bud is a tiny flower or leaf.
These are next year's flowers and leaves.
They will bloom or spread
next spring.

The history of a tree
from tiny acorn to mature oak.
On a fall day long ago, near the
base of a rock outcrop, a gray
squirrel buried one of many
acorns as a winter food source.

Forgotten by the squirrel, the
acorn sprouts in spring. By
summer's end the oak tree
is eight to ten inches tall.

After two years, at about two feet
tall, the sapling grows out of the
rock's shadow and spreads its
leaves to gather sunlight.

At about twenty years old and twenty-four
feet tall, the tree grows above
the rock. Many birds, mammals,
and insects live on the young oak.

Age and growth rings.
Cambium layer: a layer of cells
that forms both outer bark and
inner wood. Spring wood cells
are light in color. Summer cells
are darker.

These two growth
periods form rings that
are visible in a cut tree
trunk. By counting the
rings you can determine
the age of a tree.

At about thirty-five feet tall, the oak
tree flowers for the first time,
as its branches mature into limbs.
Upward growth now slows, but
spread and girth growth continue.

At more than sixty feet tall, the mature
white oak tree spreads over the
rock outcrop where the gray
squirrel buried the acorn so many
years ago. Through season after
season of heat, cold, rain, drought,
and disease, the oak has flowered
every spring, leafed every
summer, and dropped its acorns
every fall. The tree has provided
thousands of birds, mammals, and
insects with food and shelter.

Autumn has arrived, and the days are
growing shorter and cooler. The
full-grown acorns fall from the tree.
The leaves are changing color.
Soon most of them will also fall.
It's time for plants and animals to prepare
for winter. Some, like the
red-tailed hawks, may fly away;
others, like the skunks, grow a warm
winter coat. The squirrels store seeds
and nuts; the oak and other trees
will sleep through the winter.
The oak tree prepares to
sleep by moving less sap
from its roots
and stem.

Autumn colors.
As the days of autumn grow shorter, there is less sunlight.
The decrease in sunlight causes a decrease in transpiration
(water movement). When there is less light and water,
the photosynthesis process slows, causing
the leaves to change color.
Falling leaves.
When the water movement slows, a layer of cells
called the abscission layer forms between the
leafstalk and the twig. When this
layer forms completely, it stops the water
supply and the leaves fall off. Some oak leaves,
however, hold on through winter.
Sleeping trees.
A reduction in transpiration causes a decrease in sap
(food) flow, so tree growth slows. When transpiration
and sap flow cease altogether, the tree stops growing.
The oak now sleeps or rests through winter.

Flying squirrel.
9½ inches long. A flying squirrel doesn't fly —
it glides. A layer of loose skin
along its sides between the wrists
and ankles and a broad flat tail make it
possible for this unique animal to glide
from tree to tree or tree to ground.
It may glide as far as 150 feet.
The flying squirrel is common but nocturnal
(active at night), so it is seldom seen.
Its large eyes aid it with night vision.
Food includes nuts, fruit, insects, and hatchling birds.

All around the hill the green leaves
of summer have changed
to the many colors of fall.

After the downy woodpeckers
raise their family, they leave
their nest hole. A flying squirrel
moves in and makes its home.
On a cool, clear night, the
flying squirrel leaps from
its hole in the oak tree.

Beech family.
Oaks are members of the Fagaceae family.
All members, including beeches and chestnuts,
have shell-covered nuts and alternate leaves.

About sixty species of oaks are found across the
United States. The map shows some of the oaks and a
few of the many animals that use them for food and shelter.

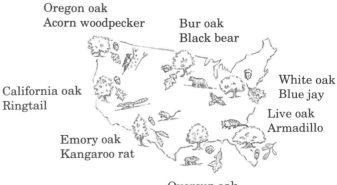

Oregon oak
Acorn woodpecker

Bur oak
Black bear

California oak
Ringtail

White oak
Blue jay

Live oak
Armadillo

Emory oak
Kangaroo rat

Overcup oak
Collared peccary

A woolly bear caterpillar wriggles across a colorful oak leaf. Oak bullet galls form on the twigs. And the old tree moves less and less sap as each passing day grows shorter and colder.

Woolly bear.
The woolly bear is the caterpillar of the Isabella moth.
It is the most common caterpillar of the fall season.

The woolly bear spends the winter curled in a ball under forest litter. In spring it forms a cocoon. The adult moth emerges, mates, and lays its eggs. Caterpillars hatch in late summer.

Folklore: the wider the black bands on the woolly bear's ends, the severer the winter will be. This is a myth; the black bands indicate the woolly bear's age. Young caterpillars have more black than older ones, and they are more likely to be seen as winter draws near.

Gall.
A protective ball of tissue that forms on a twig or a leaf. It is a plant's reaction to an irritation, usually caused by an insect.

The oak bullet gall may develop when the tiny gall wasp, less than one-eighth of an inch long, lays its eggs in an oak twig. The wasp's larva hatches inside the gall and feeds on the plant's juices. The larva tunnels to the surface, pupates (changes) into an adult wasp, and breaks out of the gall.

By now the oak has dropped most of its acorns.
Its leaves fall, covering many of the acorns.
A pair of turkeys comes to the oak to feed on
fallen acorns. Through autumn and winter
they will return again and again.

The weather has turned cold. Leaves cover the ground. Evening falls, and an opossum sets out from its root den behind the oak, in search of food. The old tree slips deeper into sleep.

The robin's nest has been empty for many weeks. Soon it may break apart. But a white-footed mouse covers the nest with a roof of grass and weeds. After storing seeds and nuts in the nest, the mouse moves in for the winter.

Opossum.
About 31 inches long, including its tail.

The opossum is the only North American marsupial. The mother carries her half-inch-long under-developed young in her external pouch until they are fully developed.

The opossum has a prehensile tail, which it uses to grip, climb, carry leaves, and make a nest.
When threatened, it may "play possum," pretending to be dead until the threat ends. Be careful: opossums may bite.

White-footed mouse.
6 to 7 inches long, including its tail.

It nests anyplace — under a log, in a bird's nest, a root hollow, or a building. Stores a food cache to help it survive the long winter months.
It breeds from March to November, producing two to four litters per year, with up to six young per litter.

Weeks pass, and a light snow falls over the hills,
the first snow of winter.
The gray squirrel is cozy in its nest.
The honeybees cluster in their hive.
A ruffed grouse scratches in the snow and
leaves for acorns, and a flying squirrel
peeks from its hole to see
what the noise is all about.
Now the old tree is once again
deep in sleep.

The sun's effect.
The tilt of the earth on its axis as it travels around
the sun determines the amount of sunlight striking an
area. Sunlight, and lack of it, causes seasonal changes
and affects the behavior of plants and animals.

Summer.
The sun rises earlier,
travels higher
(sunlight strikes more
directly), and sets later;
days are long and hot.

Winter.
The sun rises later,
travels lower
(sunlight strikes indirectly),
and sets earlier;
days are short and cold.

Dormancy.
A deep sleep. To survive the cold winter months, many living things slow or suspend some of their physical processes.

Cecropia moth. In the fall the caterpillar weaves a silk cocoon around itself. In spring the moth, which is 5 to 6 inches long, emerges.

The black bear winters in a cave, root hollow, thicket, or brush pile. Females may give birth during dormancy.

The box turtle winters in a burrow as far as two feet below the surface.

The tent caterpillar overwinters as an egg mass on a twig. In spring the caterpillars weave triangular webs.

It's midwinter, and a blanket of snow covers the land. The old tree has been dormant, deep in sleep, for many weeks. A white-tailed deer and her two yearlings come to the hilltop to visit the oak. They will paw through the snow for acorns and tender buds and twigs from oak saplings.

The cocoon of a cecropia moth is attached to a twig. Inside the cocoon, the moth, like the oak, waits for spring.

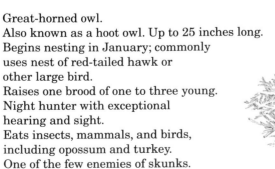

A month passes, and
the days slowly become
longer and a little warmer.
A pair of great-horned owls has
moved into the empty hawks' nest.
The female owl has laid two eggs.
Her mate brings her food while
she keeps the eggs warm and dry.

Great-horned owl.
Also known as a hoot owl. Up to 25 inches long.
Begins nesting in January; commonly
uses nest of red-tailed hawk or
other large bird.
Raises one brood of one to three young.
Night hunter with exceptional
hearing and sight.
Eats insects, mammals, and birds,
including opossum and turkey.
One of the few enemies of skunks.

After another month of warming days, spring returns. Once again
the old oak awakens from its long winter's rest and
moves sap water to its twigs and buds.
Soon flowers will bloom and leaves will unfurl.
But today something special happens.
In the leaf litter, near the roots of the old tree,
an acorn shell splits open. From inside the
shell a tiny shoot reaches out and down.
Twisting and poking, it pushes into a warm,
soft patch of soil and takes root.

Baby tree.
An oak embryo. Inside an acorn shell is a tiny tree
with two round, plump "seed leaves" full of stored fat, starch,
and protein — enough food to give a baby tree a good start on life.
When light and temperature conditions are right, the shell cracks
open. A tiny shoot called a tap root reaches down,
penetrates the soil, and starts to grow, rooting itself to that
spot for life. A stem grows from between the two leaves; this stem is
the terminal bud, or growing point of the tree, and will grow for
as long as the tree lives. Of the thousands of acorns produced by a
single tree, in a good season only a few may survive to grow into oaks.

Soon a tiny stem sprouts up and out of the shell,
and a baby oak tree begins to grow.